Child
Coll
J
639
CON

Conklin, Gladys c.2

I caught a lizard

DATE DUE

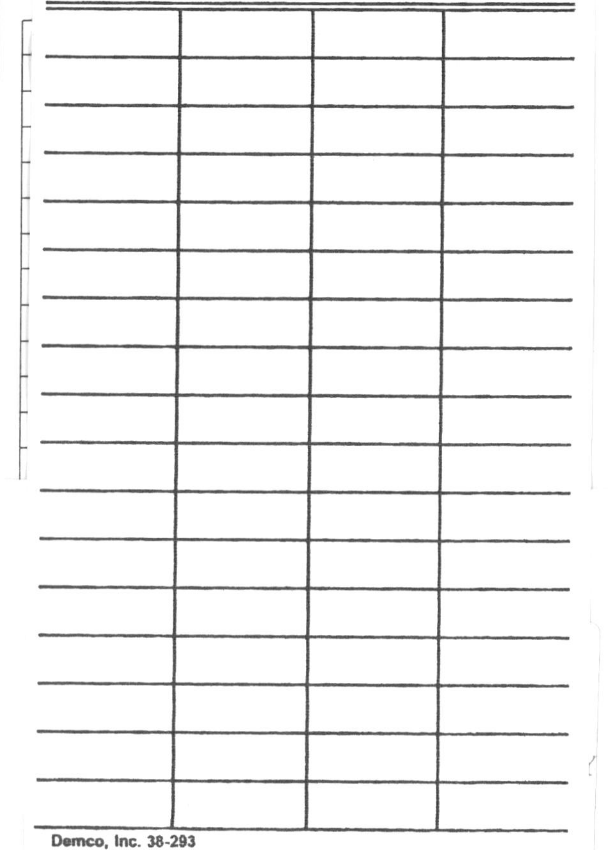

Demco, Inc. 38-293

© THE BAKER & TAYLOR CO.

OTHER BOOKS BY GLADYS CONKLIN

I LIKE CATERPILLARS
Pictures by Barbara Latham

I LIKE BUTTERFLIES
Pictures by Barbara Latham

WE LIKE BUGS
Pictures by Artur Marokvia

IF I WERE A BIRD
Pictures by Artur Marokvia

THE BUG CLUB BOOK

I Caught a Lizard

words by Gladys Conklin

pictures by Artur Marokvia

WITHDRAWN FROM
Curric Center
J. EUGENE SMITH LIBRARY
EASTERN CONN. STATE UNIVERSITY
WILLIMANTIC, CT 06226-2295

Holiday House · New York

For Cathy, David, Rickey, and Ronnie

Text copyright © 1967 by Gladys Conklin

Illustrations copyright © 1967 by Artur Marokvia

All rights reserved

Printed in the United States of America

AUTHOR'S NOTE

All children want and should have a pet of some kind. One of the first live things that a child can pick up and hold in his hand is a caterpillar—usually the black woolly kind because it can be found nearly everywhere. It's a good pet to start with. Put one in a jar, feed it, and watch it grow and change. Clean the jar and put in fresh food every day. If you can't remember to do this, then the caterpillar should be turned loose.

This book presents other small wild pets that you can find and enjoy. It tells where to look for them and how to take care of them. A page at the end of the book lists the kinds of foods these insects and other small animals like to eat.

The whole outdoors is full of exciting things to explore and observe. You cannot start too young.

—Gladys Conklin

I was standing beside a rock
when I saw him. He was a small
gray lizard. I thought he was
sleeping in the sun.
A big, buzzy fly landed in front of him.
Quick as a flash,
He caught that fly and swallowed it.
I wanted that lizard.

I moved closer and closer,
like a shadow growing bigger.
I inched my hand over the rock
and quickly grabbed him around
the head and front legs.
I held him up. He was a blue-belly.
A real blue-belly.

His dry, scaly skin tickled my hand.
His long, pointed tail whipped
back and forth. I held him carefully.
I didn't want to break that beautiful tail.
Another tail would take a long time
to grow, and it would be crooked.

I put my lizard in an empty fish bowl
with some warm sand and a piece of wood.
Every day I'll feed him a live grasshopper
or a small worm or a fat spider.
When I get tired of feeding my lizard,
I'll take him back to that rock
where I found him. He can catch his own
grasshoppers, and I can sit and watch him.

After a rain I go hunting
for salamanders. I look under rocks
and boards. Once I found a red one.
He sat in the center of my hand
and seemed to like it there.
I like salamanders, because they do not
bite or scratch or sting.

Salamanders are soft and wet.
I don't pick them up. I let them crawl
on and off my hand. I'm very careful,
because I don't want to hurt them.
I'll take mine to school to show my class.
Then I'll take him back where I found him
and turn him loose. He will be happier
in his natural home.

It rained hard last night.
The wind blew and made a big noise.
It broke several branches in my swing tree.
Under the tree, I found a baby bird.
It was cold and wet and making small sounds.
I picked it up carefully in both hands
and ran to the house.

I made a nest of soft paper.
Almost every hour I fed the baby bird.
It liked hard-boiled egg yolk and
bits of hamburger. Its feathers grew out,
and one day it flew across the room.
I didn't keep it any longer.
A wild bird must never be caged.
It needs the whole outdoors in which to fly.

I stood still and squished the warm sand
between my toes. In front of me
there was a horned toad in the sand.
I could see the top of his head and two eyes.
I scooped him up in my hands. I held him
level with my face and squinted my eyes.
The horns on his head looked bigger and
bigger. He looked like a dinosaur.

I won't keep my horned toad very long.
He isn't happy in a small pan or box.
His favorite food is ants, and he
likes to hunt for them himself.
I'll keep him two or three days
to watch him. Then I'll take him back
where I found him. I'll turn him loose,
because I like him.

The big boy next door gave me
a garter snake. He showed me how
to pick a snake up and hold him.
I'm not afraid of his black tongue
that darts in and out.
He doesn't sting with it.
It helps him smell things.

My snake feels soft and dry
around my neck. I like to hold him and
feel his scaly skin slide through my hands.
I put live earthworms in his cage.
Sometimes snakes won't eat when they are
penned up. If my snake doesn't eat
in a week, I'll take him to a grassy field.
He needs to be free to hunt for his own food.

We went to the county fair.
I bought a small, green chameleon
and some mealworms to feed him.
He also eats live grasshoppers and
small moths and flies. I like to watch
him drink water out of a bottle cap.

A chameleon looks like a lizard,
but he has a special magic.
Sometimes he is green.
When I look another time, he is brown.
I don't know how he does it.
I wish I could change color the way he does.
I would lie down in the green grass,
and no one could see me.

I saved my pennies and bought
a turtle at the pet shop.
I have a round turtle-pan with
an island in the middle.
My turtle can swim in the water
or crawl out to sit in the sun.
On warm days I put his dish outdoors,
half in the sun and half in the shade.

My turtle knows me. Every morning at eight o'clock I tap on the side of his bowl. He sticks his head up and waits for food. I feed him once a day. He likes fresh lettuce, tiny bits of beef, or turtle food. I like to play with my turtle. I like to hold him in my hand while we look at each other. I put him on the floor and let him crawl around.

I found a praying mantis
sitting on a leaf.
She crawled up on my finger
and looked at me. She stayed
there all the way home.
I put her in a large glass cage
with a few sticks and green branches.
A screen top keeps her there so she
won't get lost in the house.

I catch live grasshoppers for her,
and crickets and katydids and caterpillars.
Sometimes I give her small pieces of fresh
liver on a toothpick. I like to watch her
clean each tiny spine on her two front legs.
And she washes her face just like my cat.
If I want to, I can put her in the garden,
and she will catch her own food.

There's a big, fat toad in our rose garden. He hides under the leaves during the day. At night he roams around hunting for food. He eats beetles and moths and fireflies. And slugs and sow bugs and earthworms. We like to have him in our garden.

I never take the toad out
of the garden. I like to put my hands
around him and feel his rough, warty skin.
But he does not make warts on my hands.
I never see him during the winter.
He digs a hole and sleeps deep under
the earth. When the days get warm,
I start looking for him.

There's a big black and yellow spider in our garden. Sometimes I run right through her web, and it's all over my face. But the next morning the web is whole again. It looks like magic.

If I stand still, I can watch the spider spinning her web. Once I saw a fly get caught. The spider wrapped her web around and around the fly. I never put a spider in a jar. She wouldn't have room to spin her beautiful web. I leave her in the garden to catch flies and other bugs.

I walked across a newly plowed field and found a baby cottontail rabbit. I couldn't leave him there. I think his nest had been run over by a tractor. I was careful not to hurt him, but he was scared. I could feel his heart beating against my hands.

I took him home and put him in a big warm basket. I used a doll's bottle to give him warm milk. He nursed eagerly and also nibbled on a fresh lettuce leaf. Soon he was eating peanuts and carrots. It was time to turn him loose. I took him back to the field where other rabbits live. He hopped away into the bushes, and I was glad he was free.

Once I caught a dragonfly.
It was sitting still
on a dead branch.
I crept closer and dropped my net
over it. It was a beautiful
sparkling green. I didn't want
to keep it. I wanted a close look
at its ferocious face.

A dragonfly has a big mouth
that chews up mosquitoes. Two large
eyes bulge out on the sides of its head.
Its wings are as fine as fairy-thin glass.
They don't look strong enough to carry
a rushing dragonfly all summer.
But they do. I opened my net and swish!
Away it flew.

Down by the pond near our house
I found a round mass of clear frog eggs.
I dipped them up in a jar with plenty
of water and took them home.
When they hatch, I will keep about ten tadpoles.
I'll take the others back to the pond,
so they can grow up and make more frogs.

As the tadpoles grow bigger, bumps show where their legs will be. I watch and watch but never see the legs pop out of the skin. When they have four legs, I put a board in the water. They like to sit out of the water part of the time. When the last bit of tail disappears, I take the frogs down to the pond. It's a better home than I can give them. I can come back often and watch them splash into the water and swim away.

One summer we went camping in the woods. A big squirrel with a bushy tail came right up close to me. I stood still, and he took a piece of bread from my fingers. Then he ran back to a tree to eat it.

I wanted to catch him
and take him home. But he
wouldn't be happy in a cage.
Even a big tree isn't enough room
for a squirrel. He needs a whole forest
to race through.

I found some minnows in the brook. I dipped up a few in a can and brought them home. They looked very pretty in our fish bowl. But I don't think they liked living in a fish bowl.

They ate the fish food that I sprinkled on the water. But in a few days their bright colors began to fade. Soon they had no color at all. I took them back to the brook where I found them. I'll watch them in the brook and keep goldfish in the fish bowl.

I like all the small creatures
that I find outdoors.
I like to hold them and feel
them and look at them.
I like to keep them in my room
in a box or a jar. For two or three
days they seem happy in a cage.

After a few days, some of them
sit and stare at me.
I stare at them and I think —
I wouldn't want to be locked up
in a strange place. I know it's time
to take them back where I found them.
I turn them loose and watch them
swiftly disappear.

FOOD REQUIREMENTS

Baby Birds	Hardboiled egg yoke mixed with bread and moistened in milk. Bits of hamburger.
Chameleons	Live flies, moths, grasshoppers, mealworms.
Dragonflies	Mosquitoes, which they must catch themselves.
Frogs	Live grasshoppers, moths, beetles, earthworms, bits of raw meat.
Horned Toads	Live ants, flies, mealworms.
Lizards	Live flies, moths, mealworms, ants, grasshoppers.
Minnows	Dried fish food.
Praying Mantis	Live insects, mealworms, bits of raw liver offered on end of toothpick.
Baby Rabbits	Warm milk from nursing bottle, lettuce.
Salamanders	Live earthworms, water insects, dried turtle food.
Snakes	Live earthworms, bits of raw meat waved in front of snake's face.
Spiders	Live flies, moths, other insects.
Squirrels	Almonds, walnuts, bread.
Tadpoles	Water plants, cooked spinach, dried fish food.
Toads	Live moths, beetles, fireflies, earthworms.
Turtles	Dried turtle food, lettuce, bits of beef, live insects, worms.